Parenting
Part Guerrilla Warfare

celebrating the delights and challenges of parenting

PuddleDancer PRESS™

Created by Meiji Stewart

Illustrated by David Blaisdell

Parenting: Part Joy, Part Guerrilla Warfare
© 1997 by Meiji Stewart

ISBN# 0-9647349-6-6

PuddleDancer Press is an imprint of the
Keep Coming Back Company.
Published in Del Mar, California
P.O. Box 1204, Del Mar, California 92014
1-800-522-3383

1st Printing

Illustration: David Blaisdell, Tucson, Arizona
Cover design: Kahn Design, Encinitas, California
Book design: Roger Krueger, San Diego, California
Printing: Dickinson Press, Grand Rapids, Michigan

Dedicated to my family, who mean the world to me:
My mother, Nanette, and father, Richard, my grandmother
Mary, my sister, Leslie, my brothers, Ray and Scott, my
nephews and nieces Sebastien, Emilie, Skye, Luke, Jake,
Nanette, Cairo and Kamana, and to Fumi, Jocelyne, Richard
and Stephen. And especially to my daughter Malia (the
puddledancer), and her loving mom, Julie.

Thanks to:
David for the wonderful illustrations. I am truly blessed to be
able to work with him. Thanks also to Roger for putting it all
together, almost always under deadline (usually yesterday).
Thanks to Jeff for the delightful book covers, and, even more,
for his friendship. Thanks to Zane, Regina, Jan, Gay and Jane
for all you do and for being so loving and caring. And a very
special thanks to my mom and dad for encouraging me to
believe in and pursue my dreams.

Children make the world special
just by being in it.

Cooked Carrots:
On way to mouth, drop in lap.
Smuggle to garbage in napkin.

Delia Ephron

Spinach: Divide into little piles. Rearrange again into new piles. After five or six maneuvers, sit back and say you are full. *Delia Ephron*

There are three ways to get something done:
do it yourself, hire someone,
or forbid your kids to do it.

Monta Crane

There is nothing more important
than to take time, spend time and
give time to your children.

The world tips away when we look in our children's faces. *Louise Erdrich*

The little girl had the making of a
poet in her who, being told to be
sure of her meaning before she
spoke, said, "How can I know what
I think till I see what I say?"

Graham Wallas

The easiest way to convince my
kids that they don't really need
something is to get it for them.

Joan Collins

For children is there any happiness
which is not also noise? *Frederick W. Faber*

Children are the purpose of life.
We were once children and
someone cared for us.
Now it is our time to care.

A Cree Elder

A child will make love stronger,
days shorter, nights longer,
bankrolls smaller, homes happier,
clothes shabbier, the past forgotten,
and the future worth living.

To show a child what has once delighted you,
to find the child's delight added to your own,
so that there is now a double delight seen in the
glow of trust and affection, this is happiness. *J. B. Priestley*

The Right:
To affection, love and understanding. To adequate nutrition and medical care. To fine education.
To full opportunity for play and recreation. To a name and nationality. To special care, if handicapped.
To be among the first to receive relief in times of disaster. To learn to be a useful member of society and to develop individual abilities. To be brought up in a spirit of peace and universal brotherhood.
To enjoy these rights, regardless of race, color, sex, religion, national or social origin.

UN Declaration of the Rights of the Child

People who say they sleep like a baby usually don't have one. *Leo J. Burke*

A little girl was late arriving home from
school, so the mother asked her why:
"I had to help another girl. She was in
trouble," replied the daughter.
"What did you do to help her?"
"Oh, I sat down and helped her cry."

To be a child is to
know the joy of living.
To love a child is to
know the beauty of life.

Whenever we take trip, we have to enlist the help of thirteen sherpas, a chauffeur, two maids and a nanny— and that's only for the baby's luggage. *Ginger Hinchman*

Babies are bits of stardust
blown from the hand of God.

Larry Barretto

We should not make light
of the troubles of children.
They are worse than ours,
because we can see
the end of our trouble
and they can never see any end.

William Middleton

Do everything right, all the time, and the child will prosper. It's as simple as that, except for fate, luck, heredity, chance, and the astrological sign under which the child was born, his order of birth, his first encounter with evil, the girl who jilts him in spite of his excellent qualities, the war that is being fought when he is a young man, the drugs he may try once or too many times, the friends he makes, how he scores on tests, how well he endures kidding about his shortcomings, how ambitious he becomes, how far he falls behind, circumstantial evidence, ironic perspective, danger when it's least expected, difficulty in triumphing over circumstance, people with hidden agendas, and animals with rabies.

Ann Beattie

The one most important thing kids need to help them survive in this world is someone who's crazy about them.

Urie Bronfenbrenner

I never understood why babies were created with all the component parts necessary for a rich, full life. . . with the unfinished plumbing left to amateurs. If it was a matter of money, there isn't a mother in this world who wouldn't have chipped in a few extra bucks to have the kid completely assembled, trained, and ready to take on long trips.

Erma Bombeck

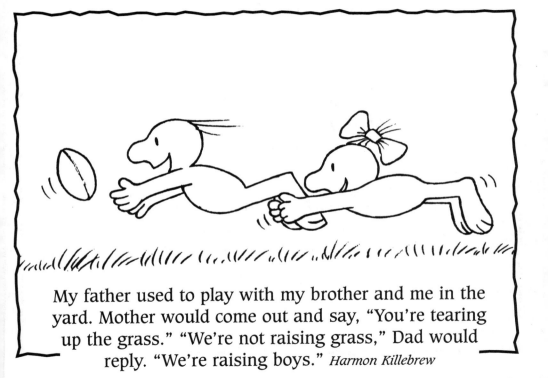

My father used to play with my brother and me in the yard. Mother would come out and say, "You're tearing up the grass." "We're not raising grass," Dad would reply. "We're raising boys." *Harmon Killebrew*

It goes without saying that you
should never have more children
than you have car windows.

Erma Bombeck

Adolescence is that period in
a kid's life when his or her
parents become more difficult.

Ryan O'Neal

The best things you can give children, next to good habits, are good memories. *Sydney Harris*

Yes, having a child is surely the
most beautifully irrational act that
two people in love can commit.

Bill Cosby

The most important thing in the world is that
you make yourself the greatest, grandest,
most wonderful loving person in the world
because this is what you are going to be giving
to your children—to all those you meet.

Leo Buscaglia

You never really understand a person until you consider things from their point of view. *Harper Lee*

Do you know why grown-ups are always asking little kids what they want to be when they grow up? It's because they're looking for ideas.

Paula Poundstone

A child enters your home and for the next twenty years makes so much noise you can hardly stand it. The child departs, leaving the house so silent you think you are going to go mad.

John Andrew Holmes

We've had bad luck with our kids; they've all grown up.

Christopher Morley

When I became a father,
I learned that insanity in children,
like radio transmission,
is liveliest at night.

Bill Cosby

As we read the school reports upon our
children, we realize with a sense of relief that
can rise to delight that—thank Heavens—
nobody is reporting in this fashion upon us.

J. B. Priestley

You cannot teach a child to take care of himself
unless you will let him try to take care of himself.
He will make mistakes; and out of these
mistakes will come his wisdom. *Henry Ward Beecher*

If evolution really works,
how come mothers
have only two hands?

Ed Dussault

I have found the happiness of
parenthood greater than any
other that I have experienced.

Bertrand Russell

What the mother sings to the cradle goes all the way to the grave. *Henry Ward Beecher*

Children Are...

Amazing, acknowledge them. • Believable, trust them.
Childlike, allow them. • Divine, honor them. • Energetic,
nourish them. • Fallible, embrace them. • Gifts, treasure
them. • Here Now, be with them. • Innocent, delight
with them. • Joyful, appreciate them. • Kindhearted,
learn from them. • Lovable, cherish them. • Magical, fly
with them. • Noble, esteem them. • Open minded,
respect them. • Precious, value them. • Questioners,
encourage them. • Resourceful, support them.
Spontaneous, enjoy them. • Talented, believe in them.
Unique, affirm them. • Vulnerable, protect them.
Whole, recognize them. • Xtraspecial, celebrate them.
Yearning, notice them. • Zany, laugh with them.

© Meiji Stewart

A child is the greatest poem ever known.

Christopher Morley

If you were arrested for being a loving parent,
would there be enough evidence to convict you?

Here we have a baby.
It is composed of a bald head
and a pair of lungs.

Eugene Field

Attaching high value to a child
means being attentive and responsive
to that child's needs.

Gary Smalley & John Trent

When I was a kid, I used to imagine animals running under by bed. I told my dad, and he solved the problem by cutting the legs off the bed. *Lou Brock*

A characteristic of the normal child is
that he doesn't act that way very often.

Franklin P. Jones

When you give your children material things
as replacements for love,
you teach them that it is objects, not love,
which will bring them happiness.

Barbara De Angelis

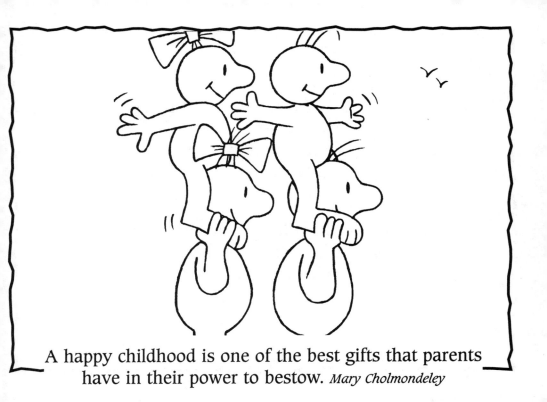

A happy childhood is one of the best gifts that parents have in their power to bestow. *Mary Cholmondeley*

If you make children happy now,
you will make them happy
twenty years hence
by the memory of it.

Kate Douglas Wiggin

A young child, a fresh, uncluttered mind,
a world before him—to what treasures
will you lead him?

Gladys M. Hunt

A child should not be denied a balloon because an adult knows that sooner or later it will be burst. *Marcelen Cox*

Encouraging a child means that one or more
of the following critical life messages are
coming through, either by word or by action:
I believe in you, I trust you, I know you can handle this.
You are listened to, you are cared for,
you are very important to me.

Barbara Coloroso

Allow children to be happy their own way;
for what better way will they ever find?

Dr. Samuel Johnson

Let you kids play in the mud. The mud will wash off, but the memories will last a lifetime. *R. D. Ramsey*

Never give advice to your children
unless you have it in writing and notarized.

Marshall Rosenberg

If you must hold yourself up to
your children as an object lesson. . .
hold yourself up as an example
and not as a warning.

G. B. Shaw

The kind of man who thinks that helping with the dishes is beneath him will also think that helping with the baby is beneath him, and then he certainly is not going to be a very successful father. *Eleanor Roosevelt*

I guess the real reason that my wife and
I had children is the same reason that
Napoleon had for invading Russia:
it seemed like a good idea at the time.

Bill Cosby

Babies: A loud noise at one end and
no sense of responsibility at the other.

Father Ronald Knox

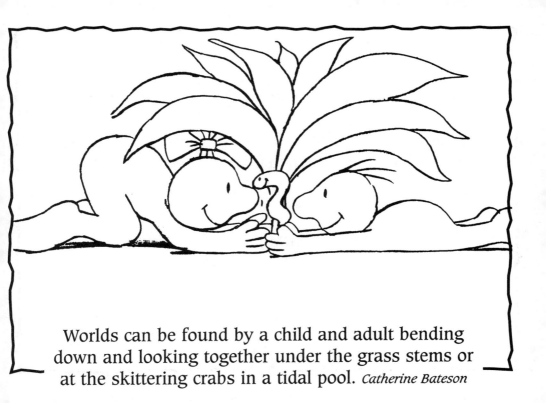

Worlds can be found by a child and adult bending down and looking together under the grass stems or at the skittering crabs in a tidal pool. *Catherine Bateson*

Too often we underestimate the power of a touch,
a smile, a kind word, a listening ear,
an honest compliment, or the smallest act of caring,
all of which have the potential to turn a life around.

Leo Buscaglia

The fundamental job of a toddler is
to rule the universe.

Lawrence Kutner

In the event of an oxygen shortage on airplanes, mothers of young children are always reminded to put on their own oxygen mask first, to better assist the children with theirs. The same tactic is necessary on terra firma. There's no way of sustaining our children if we don't first rescue ourselves. I don't call that selfish behavior. I call it love.

Joyce Manyard

Teenagers are people who express a burning desire to be different by dressing exactly alike.

If your children know from the earliest days that you love them no matter what—you'll probably do just fine. Taking the time now to build the proper foundation by entering your child's world and understanding how he or she feels and thinks, and by talking, laughing, playing, and just being together, may be the best investment you will ever make in the future of your family.

Jane Nelsen

Each day of our lives we make deposits in the memory banks of our children.

Charles R. Swindoll

Children are not so different from kites—they were created to fly. But they need wind—the undergirding and strength that comes from unconditional love, encouragement and prayer. *Gigi Graham Tchividjian*

The most important medicine is tender love and care.

Mother Teresa

Fifty years from now, it will not matter
what kind of car you drove, what kind of
house you lived in, how much you had in
your bank account nor what your clothes
looked like. But the world will be a little
better because you were important in the
life of a child.

Speak up for all the children.

With two sons born eighteen months apart, I operated mainly on automatic pilot through the ceaseless activity of their early childhood. I remember opening the refrigerator late one night and finding a roll of aluminum foil next to a pair of small red tennies. Certain that I was responsible for the refrigerated shoes, I quickly closed the door and ran upstairs to make sure I had put the babies in their cribs instead of the linen closet.

Mary Kay Blakely

If you want to recapture your youth,
just cut off his allowance.

Al Berstein

Listening children know stories are there.
When their elders sit and begin, children are
just waiting and hoping for one to come out,
like a mouse from a hole. *Eudora Welty*

By the way, many people make the false assumption that because a baby can't speak he can't hear. As a result, when confronted with an infant, any infant, they raise their voices and speak very distinctly, as though they were ordering a meal in a foreign language.

Jean Kerr

The love I feel for my child is like a balloon that keeps filling up and expanding. It never bursts, it just keeps getting bigger and bigger. Maybe, over a lifetime, the love will fill many balloons!

Judy Schmidt

There are many little ways to enlarge your child's world.
Love of books is the best of all. *Jacqueline Kennedy Onassis*

We should seize every opportunity
to give encouragement.
Encouragement is oxygen to the soul.

George M. Adams

Children thrive in a variety of family forms;
they develop normally with single parents,
with unmarried parents, with multiple caretakers in
a communal setting, and with traditional two-parent
families. What children require is loving and
attentive adults, not a particular family type.

Sandra Scarr

It takes an entire village to raise a child.
African proverb

One of the most obvious facts about grownups to a child is that they have forgotten what it is like to be a child.

Randall Jarrell

Children are among the most conscious, most loving, most accepting, most happy, most trusting, most honest, most intuitive, most wise people in the universe.
How can we not treat them
with respect and dignity?

It is easier to build strong children than to repair broken men. *Frederick Douglass*

My mother was the making of me.
She was so true and so sure of me,
I felt that I had someone to live for—
someone I must not disappoint.
The memory of my mother will
always be a blessing to me.

Thomas A. Edison

Fatherhood, for me, has been less a job than an
unstable and surprising combination of adventure,
blindman's bluff, guerrilla warfare and crossword puzzle.

Frederick F. Van De Water

Nobody's family can hang out the sign,
"Nothing the matter here."

Chinese proverb

Children will do what they need to do
when they are ready—
they cannot do things until then—
enjoy them, don't worry.
Let them tell you when they're ready for more.
Enjoy your children's childhood—
it doesn't last long.

There are only two things
a child will share willingly—
communicable diseases
and his mother's age.

Dr. Benjamin Spock

All children running loose
and unattended will be towed
away at owner's expense.

All elders should have at least one youngster to be "crazy about" and vice versa. Grandparenting supplies the role model for a healthy and fulfilling old age. And grandchildren want grandparents. *Arthur Kornhaber, M.D.*

Hit pillows, never kids.

An eminent baby specialist had a standard treatment for weak newborn infants who failed to gain weight. When he came to the baby's chart during his rounds in the hospital, he always noted the following direction to the nurse in attendance: "This baby is to be loved every three hours."

To let your kids take responsibility is to allow them to feel good about themselves. *Maria Montessori*

Parenthood is one of the last frontiers.

Phil Batchelor

Never, EVER serve
sugary snacks on
rainy days.

No day is so bad it can't be fixed with a nap.

Don't limit your child to your own learning,
for he was born in another time.

Rabbinical saying

You are the molders of their dreams. . .
the spark that sets aflame the poet's hand
or lights the flame in some great singer's song.

Clark Mollenhoff

Gender equity means boys need to cook, and girls need to hammer.

I remember leaving the hospital... thinking:
"Wait, are they going to let
me just walk off with him?
I don't know beans about babies!"

Anne Tyler

Though motherhood is the most important of all
the professions—requiring more knowledge than
any other department in human affairs—there was
not attention given to preparation for this office.

Elizabeth Cady Stanton

A hug delights and warms and charms;
it must be why we were given arms.

If we are not sure whether what we are doing with children is right, we need only to put ourselves in their place and ask if we would want it done to us—not was it done to us, but would we want it done to us? If the answer is no, then we have to ask ourselves why we would ever want to do it to our children.

Barbara Coloruso

Childhood is that wonderful period when all
you need to do to lose weight is to take a bath.

Children Need:

Appreciation, for all they bring into our lives.
Balance, somewhere between too little and too much.
Commitment, it takes a village to raise a child. • Dreams,
to touch the future. • Empathy, remember what it was
like to be a child. • Family and Friends, everyone needs
someone to love. • Guidance, actions speak louder than
words. • Healthy Habits, to nurture body, mind and
spirit. • Inspiration, explore the world of music, books,
art and dance. • Joy, sprinkle laughter and happiness
daily. • Kindness, to learn to treat others as they are
treated. • Limits, set boundaries and consequences

together. • **Mentors**, to give wings to their aspirations. **Nature**, to discover rainbow trails and shooting stars. **Opportunities**, to feel good about themselves. • **Play**, the "work" of childhood. • **Quiet Time**, to recharge their batteries. • **Responsibilities**, to build self-esteem and self-confidence. • **Security**, feeling safe is essential for growth. **Traditions**, keep the family tree alive and sprout new branches. • **Unconditional Love**, for who they are, not for what they do. • **Values**, live yours and encourage them to find theirs. • **Words Of Encouragement**, "You can do it, I believe in you." • **Xxxooo's**, hug and kiss them each and every day. • **You**, your presence more than your presents. • **Zzzzzz's**, a good night's sleep.

Siblings:
Children of the same parents,
each of whom is perfectly normal
until they get together.

Sam Levenson

A grandchild is a miracle,
but a renewed relationship
with your own children
is even a greater one.

T. Berry Brazelton

Children in a family are like flowers in a bouquet. There's always one determined to face in an opposite direction from the way the arranger desires. *Madeline Cox*

Recognizing the good in children is one
of the greatest gifts we can give to them.

If children were allowed to run the country,
we'd have soda flowing out of the drinking fountains,
bridges built with Tinkertoys, styrofoam airliners,
and bad countries would have to play by themselves.

Walter Wandheim

Hitch your wagon to a star.

R. W. Emerson

Know you what is is to be a child? It is to believe in love, to believe in loveliness, to believe in belief; it is to be so little that the elves can reach to whisper in your ear; it is to turn pumpkins into coaches, and mice into horses, lowness into loftiness, and nothing into everything, for each child has its fairy godmother in its soul.

Francis Thompson Shelley

If you want your children to turn out well, spend twice as much time with them and half as much money on them.

Abigail Van Buren

If a child is to keep his inborn sense of wonder... he needs the companionship of at least one adult who can share it, rediscovering with him the joy, excitement and mystery of the world we live in. *Rachel Carson*

Infant care is another thing that has to
be learned from the bottom up.

Two big questions present
themselves to every parent
in one form or another:
"What kind of human being
do I want my child to become"
and "How can I go about
making that happen?"

Virginia Satir

If you see a book, a rocking chair and a grandchild in
the same room, don't pass up a chance to read aloud.
Instill in your grandchildren a love of reading.
It's one of the greatest gifts you can give. *Barbara Bush*

Self-esteem is the real magic wand that can form a child's future. A child's self-esteem affects every area of her existence, from friends she chooses, to how well she does academically in school, to what kind of job she gets, to even the person she chooses to marry.

Stephanie Marston

Children are natural mimics—they act like their parents in spite of every attempt to teach them good manners.

If you think education is expensive, try ignorance.

Derek Bok

Invest your time in the most important things in life.

Young children scare easily—a tough tone, a sharp reprimand, an exasperated glance, a peeved scowl will do it. Little signs of rejection—you don't have to hit young children to hurt them—cut very deeply.

James L. Hymes, Jr.

To fully love your children
is the beginning of a lifelong romance.

Our children are watching us live, and what we are shouts louder than anything we can say.

Wilferd A. Peterson

It is from her father that she begins to infer messages that will linger a lifetime—"I am, or am not, considered by men to be pretty, desirable, valuable, dependent, weak, strong, dim-witted, brilliant"; "Men are, or are not, trustworthy, loving, predatory, dependable, available, dangerous."

Victoria Secunda

Motherhood:
If it was going to be easy,
it never would have started
with something called labor.

The child who acts unlovable
is the child who most needs to be loved.

Cathy Rindner Tempelsman

The gain is not the
having of children;
it is the discovery of love
and how to be loving.

Polly Berrien Berends

It will be gone before you know it.
The fingerprints on the wall
appear higher and higher.
Then suddenly they disappear.

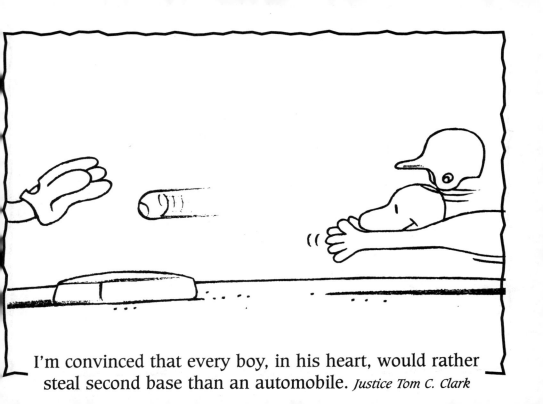

I'm convinced that every boy, in his heart, would rather steal second base than an automobile. *Justice Tom C. Clark*

Adult education
is something that will continue
as long as kids have homework.

Grown-ups never understand
anything for themselves,
and it is tiresome for
children to be always and forever
explaining things to them.

Antoine De Saint-Exupery

Every adult needs a child to teach;
that's the way adults learn. *Guy Rice Doud*

When you look at your life,
the greatest happinesses
are family happinesses.

Dr. Joyce Brothers

The best gift for any child is a
parent's undivided attention.
To be a great parent,
just take the time to really
get to know your child.

R. D. Ramsey

We awaken in others the same attitude of mind we hold towards them. *Elbert Hubbard*

If I were asked what single
qualification was necessary for one
who has the care of children,
I should say patience—
patience with their tempers,
with their understandings,
with their progress.

Francis Fenelon

When you feel like yelling,
take a five minute emergency break
and leave the room.

No quick-draw artist of the old West would stand a chance against today's grandmother with a purse full of pictures. *Frank Walsh*

A child who has never fantasized about having other parents is seriously lacking imagination.

Fred G. Gosman

Kids don't care what you think,
until they think you care.

To win the affection of children... to find the best in others... to know even one life has breathed easier because you have lived. This is to have succeeded. *Ralph Waldo Emerson*

When people ask me what I do,
I always say I am a mother first.
Your children represent your thoughts.
Your children are a statement.

Jacqueline Jackson

Nothing I've ever done has given
me more joys and rewards than
being a father to my children.

Bill Cosby

A child's hand in yours—what tenderness and power it arouses. You are instantly the very touchstone of wisdom and strength. *Marjorie Holms*

Is it not strange that he who has no
children brings them up so well?

Confucius

My parents were constantly affirming me
in everything I did. Late at night I'd wake
up and hear my mother talking over my
bed, saying, "You're going to do great on
this test. You can do anything you want."

Stephen Covey

It will be a great day when our schools get all the money they need and the Air Force has to hold a bake sale to buy a bomber.

There is nothing like having grandchildren to restore your faith in heredity.

Doug Larson

All that I am or hope to be,
I owe to my mother.

Abraham Lincoln

Children find comfort in flaws,
ignorance, insecurities similar to their own.
I love my mother for letting me see hers.

Erma Bombeck

Children can because we help them believe in themselves.

Act your age!

Stop yelling.
If you want to ask
me something, come here.
STOP YELLING.
IF YOU WANT TO ASK
ME SOMETHING, COME HERE.

Delia Ephron

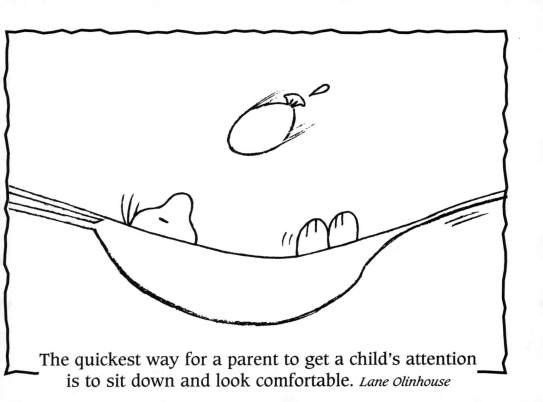

The quickest way for a parent to get a child's attention is to sit down and look comfortable. *Lane Olinhouse*

An error means a child needs help, not a
reprimand or ridicule for doing something wrong.

Marva Collins

When children are treated with respect, they
conclude that they deserve respect and hence
develop self-respect. When children are treated
with acceptance, they develop self-acceptance;
when they are cherished, they conclude that they
deserve to be loved, and they develop self-esteem.

Stephanie Marston

Children have a lot to contribute to our lives if given the chance. *Ida Nelle Hollaway*

Wherever I look, I see signs of the commandment to honor one's parents and nowhere of a commandment that calls for the respect of a child.

Alice Miller

Children are on loan from God. Pay attention to who has been sent to you for caretaking.

Barbara De Angelis

A torn jacket is soon mended, but harsh words bruise the heart of a child. *Henry Wadsworth Longfellow*

Few of us, as we run the bath water or spread the peanut butter on the bread, proclaim proudly, "I'm making my contribution to the future of the planet." But with the exception of global hunger, few jobs in the world of paychecks and promotions compare in significance to the job of parent.

Joyce Maynard

It is the obligation of all human beings to do what is right for children.

Bev Bos

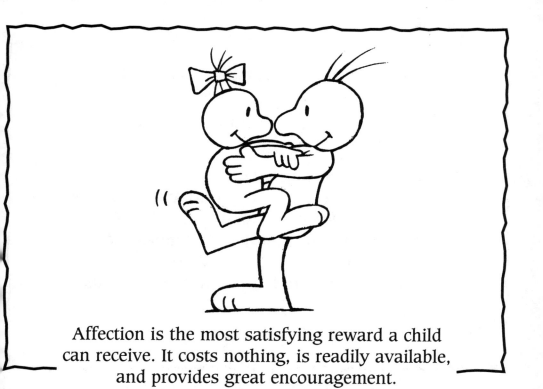

Affection is the most satisfying reward a child can receive. It costs nothing, is readily available, and provides great encouragement.

You can learn many things from children.
How much patience you have, for instance.

Franklin P. Jones

As parents, everything we do and say, as well as all
the things we forget to do or are unable to say,
will leave deep impressions on our children.
It is our responsibility to remember that,
so the impact we have will add to our
children's strength and not to their wounds.

Will Glennon

Celebrate what you want to see more of.
Tom Peters

Fathers Are...

Adventurous, enjoy them. • **B**elievable, trust them. • **C**aring, experience them. • **D**evoted, appreciate them. • **E**ncouraging, hear them. • **F**aithful, count on them. • **G**enuine, value them. **H**uman, accept them. • **I**mportant recognize them. • **J**oyful, delight with them. • **K**ind, embrace them. • **L**oving, cherish them. • **M**agical, dance with them. • **N**ecessary, be with them. **O**ptimistic, believe in them. • **P**riceless, treasure them. **Q**uirky, laugh with them. • **R**esponsible, depend on them. **S**trong, lean on them. • **T**ender, discover them. **U**nderstanding, talk to them. • **V**aluable, acknowledge them. **W**ise, listen to them. • **X**traordinary, admire them. • **Y**oung at Heart, play with them. • **Z**any, laugh with them.

© Meiji Stewart

114

There is no more vital calling or vocation for men than fathering.

John R. Troop

The good-enough father is not simply a knight in shining armor galloping to the occasional rescue; he is there through good times and bad, insisting on and delighting in his paternity every pleasurable and painful step of the way.

Victoria Secunda

A child is a gift whose worth cannot
be measured except by the heart.

Theresa Ann Hunt

Toddlers are more likely to eat healthy food
if they find it on the floor.

Jan Blaustone

The best toy is one the child creates. Take your child outside and show him how to build forts out of sticks, make boats out of paper—the possibilities are infinite.

A child of five would understand this.
Send somebody to fetch a child of five.

Groucho Marx

Water fascinates kids. They run toward it,
and they run away from it.
The love it in a lake or an ocean,
but it's a necessary evil in a bathtub.
They'll swim in it, sail on it, dangle feet in it—
but fight to keep it away from that
sacred area behind their ears.

Art Linkletter

Gardening teaches responsibility, hard work, patience, satisfaction, joy, wonderment, and respect for beauty. These are lessons everyone needs. Where else can kids learn how to make miracles and play in the mud at the same time? *R. D. Ramsey*

No matter how children came to be living with just one parent, they need to be told, again and again, that your family's configuration is the result of an adult decision or an act of fate that has nothing whatsoever to do with them.

Marge Kennedy

Even when freshly washed,
and relieved of all obvious confections,
children tend to be sticky.

Fran Leibowitz

Every baby needs a lap.
Henry Robin

We prefer to invest in buildings and
roads and superstructure and technology,
and we have forgotten how
to invest in our children.

Janet Reno

There should be no enforced respect for
grown-ups. We cannot prevent children
from thinking us fools by merely
forbidding them to utter their thoughts.

Bertrand Russell

No man is really depraved who can spend half an hour by himself on the floor playing with his little boy's electric train. *Simeon Strunsky*

The darn trouble with cleaning the house is it gets dirty the next day anyway, so skip a week if you have to. The children are the most important thing.

Barbara Bush

The smile that flickers on baby's lips when he sleeps—does anybody know where it was born? Yes, there is a rumor that a young pale beam of a crescent moon touched the edge of a vanishing autumn cloud, and there the smile was first born in the dream of a dew-washed morning.

Rabindranath Tagore

There never was a child so lovely but his mother
was glad to get him asleep. *Ralph Waldo Emerson*

You feel so much love for your first child that you wonder how you could possibly love the second one as much. Then you discover how infinite your capacity to love is.

Linda D'Agrosa

Being safe is about being seen and heard and allowed to be who you are and to speak your truth.

Rachel Naomi Remen, M. D.

It is impossible to overemphasize the immense need human beings have to be really listened to, to be taken seriously, to be understood. *Paul Tournier*

Literature is mostly about having sex
and not much about having children.
Life is the other way around.

David Dodge

Children are a great comfort in your old age—
and they help you reach it faster, too.

Lionel Kauffman.

Few things are more satisfying
than seeing your children
have teenagers of their own.

Doug Larson

Do not videotape your
child in the bathtub.
Do not name your child
after a Scandinavian deity
or any aspect of the weather.

Daniel Menaker

The best time to give children your advice is when they are young enough to believe you know what you are talking about.

Children don't walk like people... They canter, they bounce, they slither, slide, crawl, leap into the air, saunter, stand on their heads, swing from branch to branch, ...or trot like ostriches. But I seldom recall seeing a child just plain walk. They can, however, dawdle.

Phyllis McGinley

Children have never been good at listening to their elders, but they have never failed to imitate them. *James Baldwin*

As a father of two
there is a respectful question
which I wish to ask of fathers of five:
How do you happen to be still alive?

Ogden Nash

Our attitude toward the newborn child
should be one of reverence that a
spiritual being has been confined
within limits perceptible to us.

Maria Montessori

If you have knowledge, let others
light their candles for it. *Margaret Fuller*

One of the most important things
to remember about infant care is:
never change diapers in mid-stream.

Don Marquis

The best advice from my mother was a
reminder to tell my children everyday:
"Remember you are loved."

Evelyn McCormick

Give a little love to a child, and you will get a great deal back. *John Ruskin*

The guys who fear becoming fathers
don't understand that fathering
is not something perfect men do,
but something that perfects the man.
The end product of child raising
is not the child but the parent.

Frank Pittman

Count fingers, toes,
and noses, not mistakes.

There are one hundred and fifty-two distinctly different ways of holding a baby, and they are all right. *Heywood Broun*

Dad's don't need to be tall and
broad-shouldered and handsome and clever.
Love makes them so.

Pam Brown

Adults are obsolete children.

Dr. Seuss

If it seems a childish thing to do, do it in remembrance that you were a child. *Frederick Buechner*

Mothers Are...

Angels, cherish them. • Beautiful, recognize them.
Cheerleaders, hear them. • Divine, honor them.
Empowering, value them. • Fun, play with them. • Giving,
appreciate them. • Healers, thank them . • Intuitive, share
with them. • Joyful, celebrate them. • Kindhearted, receive
them. • Lovable, tell them. • Miraculous, treasure them.
Nurturing, allow them. • Optimists, believe in them.
Passionate, acknowledge them. • Quipsters, laugh with
them. • Resourceful, admire them. • Special, delight
with them. • Teachers, learn from them. • Unconditional,
love them. • Vulnerable, support them. • Wonderful,
embrace them. • Xtraspecial, prize them. • Young At
Heart, enjoy them. • Zestful, keep up with them.

Nothing else will ever make you
as happy or as sad, as proud or
as tired, as motherhood.

Ella Parsons

I know how to do anything—I'm a mom.

Roseane Barr Arnold

Perhaps nobody becomes more
competent in hitting a moving target
than a mother spoon feeding a baby.

When we set an example of
honesty, our children will be honest.
When we encircle them with love, they will be loving.
When we practice tolerance, they will be tolerant.
When we meet life with laughter and a twinkle in our
eye, they will develop a sense of humor.

Wilferd A. Peterson

To lead the people, walk behind them.

Lao-tzu

Cleaning your house while
your kids are still growing
is like shoveling the walk
before it stops snowing.

Phyllis Diller

The important thing is not so
much that every child should be
taught, as that every child should
be given the wish to learn.

John Lullock

Few things are more delightful than
grandchildren fighting over your lap. *Doug Larson*

Loving a child is a circular business.
The more you give, the more you get,
the more you want to give.

Penelope Leach

If I could say just one thing to parents,
it would be simply that a child needs someone
who believes in him no matter what he does.

Alice Keliher

146

The walks and talks we have with our two-year-olds
in red boots have a great deal to do with the
values they will cherish as adults. *Edith F. Hunter*

Snot happens.

There's no trick to
getting a kid to like you.
Just feed him cookies
and let him stay up
past his bedtime.

J.F. Niel

Raising kids is part joy and part guerrilla warfare.
Edward Asner

You cannot stop your kids from trying drugs, or even from abusing them, if that is what they decide to do. What you can do is practice honesty, equip your kids with accurate information about drugs, keep the doors of communication open by letting your kids know your love for them is unconditional, and remain nonjudgmental by creating a relationship where your kids feel safe to talk to you and get your input about their choices. When you abstain from judgments, your kids know that if they get into an abusive situation with their own experiment-ation, you will be there with honesty, love, and support that is empowering instead of enabling.

Jane Nelsen

The decisions we make now affect the seven generations of children to come. *American Indian wisdom, through Carol Pierce*

At the end of your life you will never regret
not having passed one more test,
not winning one more verdict,
or not closing one more deal.
You will regret time not
spent with a husband,
a friend, a child, or a parent.

When Mother Theresa received her
Nobel Prize, she was asked,
"What can we do to promote world peace?"
She replied, "Go home and love your family."

Life affords no greater responsibility, no greater privilege, than the raising of the next generation. *Dr. C. Everett Koop*

and other recipes for living & loving life

Thought-provoking, attitude-changing wonderful recipes on how to make the best from the "wurst" of any situation. Accepting challenges and overcoming adversity can lead to greater self-esteem, self-acceptance and self-discovery.

A uniquely illustrated "you can if you think you can" book to empower anybody – student, co-worker, relative, friend, partner, child – to aspire to, believe in, and pursue their dreams. Go for it! Life is not a dress rehearsal.

Even if you miss you'll land among the stars.

It's a Jungle Out There!

The best survival kit for living and loving in the jungle of every day life. Great line drawings and timeless truths to offer hope and encouragement for anyone facing the daily challenges of our fast-paced stress-filled society.

Happiness is a choice. Pass it on! Really knowing we all have the power to choose happiness at any moment, in any situation, is truly empowering. This book is a great reminder that happiness is found right here, right now.

Happiness is an Inside Job

Humor & wisdom celebrating the art of happiness

Children are Meant to be Seen & Heard

humor and wisdom for honoring children

A wondrous gift for anybody interested in the well-being of children. This delightfully illustrated book uses wisdom from the ages and poignant humor to encourage everyone, especially parents and teachers, to love, cherish, and honor children.

Dare to follow your heart's desire... Dare to harvest your dreams... Dare to speak your truth... Dare to nurture your spirit... An ideal gift book to encourage anybody to aspire to, believe in and pursue dreams.

Anything is Possible

Humor & wisdom for success and prosperity

Relax, God is in Charge

humor & wisdom for living and loving life

Let go and let God.
Please do not feel personally,
totally, irrevocably responsible
for everything. That's my job.
Love, God.
Help someone receive
understanding, insight and
support to face life's challenges.

God has a purpose and a plan
for you that no one else can
fulfill. You are a miracle, unique
and unrepeatable. Help someone
celebrate their spiritual nature
with this collection of
empowering and loving wisdom.

God Danced
the Day You Were Born

Humor & wisdom   for celebrating life

"Children Are…" on page 30, "Children Need…" on pages 72–73, "Fathers Are…" on page 144 and "Mothers Are…" on page 140 are part of our A-Z series of gift products.

Other A-Z titles include:

- Dare To
- Friends Are
- Happiness Is
- I Am/You Are
- Recovery Is

These unique sayings and many other empowering designs are available on a variety of items, including bookmarks, wallet cards and greeting cards. Please call for a complimentary catalog.

PuddleDancer PRESS™

P.O. Box 1204, Del Mar, California 92014
1-800-522-3383

Qty.	Title	Item #	Unit Cost	Total
	Relax, God is in Charge	BK01	6.95	
	Keep Coming Back	BK02	6.95	
	Children are Meant to be Seen & Heard	BK03	6.95	
	Shoot for the Moon	BK04	6.95	
	When Life Gives You Lemons...	BK05	6.95	
	It's a Jungle Out There	BK06	6.95	
	Parenting... Part Joy... Part Guerrilla Warfare	BK07	6.95	
	God Danced the Day You WereBorn	BK08	6.95	
	Happiness is an Inside Job	BK09	6.95	
	Anything is Possible	BK10	6.95	

	Subtotal	
Tax Help:	Shipping & Handling (info below)	
Tax on a 6.95 book is 0.54	CA residents (only) add 7.75% tax	
	Total	

PuddleDancer PRESS

Send books to:

Name _____

Address _____

City_____ State____ Zip _____

Phone (_____)_____

Payment via:

☐ Check/money order

☐ VISA   ☐ Mastercard   ☐ AMEX

Acct#_____Exp. Date _____

Signature_____

Yes! Please send me the books indicated above. Add $2.00 shipping and handling for the first book and 50¢ for each additional book. Add $2.50 extra to the total for books shipped to Canada. Overseas orders to be paid by credit card. Allow up to four weeks for delivery. Send check or money order payable to **Keep Coming Back**. No cash or C.O.D.'s, please. Prices subject to change without notice. Quantity discount available upon request.

Mail to: Keep Coming Back, P.O. Box 1204, Del Mar, California 92014
Call: Local: 619.452.1386   Fax: 619.452.2797   Toll-free **800.522.3383**

PuddleDancer PRESS™

Complimentary Catalog Available
P.O. Box 1204, Del Mar, California 92014   1-800-522-3383

PuddleDancer titles available from your favorite bookstore:

Relax, God is in Charge	ISBN 0-9647349-0-7
Keep Coming Back	ISBN 0-9647349-1-5
Children are Meant to be Seen and Heard	ISBN 0-9647349-2-3
Shoot for the Moon	ISBN 0-9647349-3-1
When Life Gives You Lemons…	ISBN 0-9647349-4-X
It's a Jungle Out There!	ISBN 0-9647349-5-8
Parenting… Part Joy… Part Guerrilla Warfare	ISBN 0-9647349-6-6
God Danced the Day You Were Born	ISBN 0-9647349-7-4
Happiness is an Inside Job	ISBN 0-9647349-8-2
Anything is Possible	ISBN 0-9647349-9-0

Acknowledgements

Every effort has been made to find the copyright owner of the material used.
However, there are a few quotations that have been impossible to trace, and we
would be glad to hear from the copyright owners of these quotations, so that
acknowledgement can be recognized in any future edition.